Addictions

Kodi Clissold

BookLeaf
Publishing

Presentation by *BookLeaf Publishing*

Web: www.bookleafpub.com

E-mail: info@bookleafpub.com

ISBN: 9789395755139

First edition 2022

DEDICATION

To two great loves of my life;

A - who taught me it isn't always Love at First Sight.

and

S - who taught me love is never gone from sight, even when we are.

PREFACE

It's been said to me many times; "With everything you've been through you could write a book" but what I didn't realise was that one was already writing itself. Writing itself in metaphors and rhymes. In late nights and very early mornings. In prose and disconnected thoughts, pieced together in seconds, drawn out for days or left lying in a drawer until fresh salt was rubbed in the wounds or new warmth radiated from within.

Contained inside these pages are the soul experiences with our human addictions, both conscious and subconscious, that have taught me more than any psychology degree ever could; The numbness that comes with alcohol, The rush from Caffeine The thrill of Sex, The highs of new Love, The urgency in the quest for Love, and the comfort and misunderstanding of our own Grief.

Pain

"Pain is Beautiful."
Said the wounded soldier to the tortured soul.

Whisper

Sometimes it's a whisper.
Sometimes it's a yell
and sometimes,
more often than not,
It's like when Alice fell.
Down the rabbit hole to wonderland,
a mixed up crazy town.
Until it's not.
The elation stops
and you feel yourself come down.

Weighed heavy in your pockets,
by Tears and crumpled bills
and yet again,
You leave with nothing
but a hate for cheapened thrills.
Running home hungover
with no more soul left to sell.
Still addicted;
Sometimes Loves a whisper
and Sometimes it's a yell.

Lost Boy

Two sides of the coin combine.
Heads and tails, with horns to match.
The tale of a lost boy
in a grown man's empty shell.
Living by the bottle
of liquid courage at its best.
It makes him switch from light to night,
when the ghost rattles the cage.
For a second you can see it sparkle,
the Halo that ignites his eyes,
then blink and have it left behind
by the shadows of pain.
Two people live as one inside,
fighting for the chance to rule.
While he struggles for the right to love,
they leave a mess within his wake.
Then, his wings can lift you higher
before he shoots you down with arrows
that wreak of vacillation
and wound the strongest of the saints;
The monster fuelled by alcohol.
The damage controlling man,
 pull you in their separate ways
as you fight for the only choice you have.
The strength to walk away

from doomed future and blessed fate.
From the verdict of too early or too late,
From the fear of loving a lost boy,
who will never want to change.

Christmas Sweater

5

Grief is an ugly Christmas Sweater.
Ill fitting and frayed at the edges.
Worn year after year;
It wraps you in its itchy embrace
somehow the most comforting thing you own
and yet when someone else might try it on,
it never quite will fit the same.

Fireworks

Laying black and quiet.
Caked in powder, left to sigh.
Aroused by breath across its neck.
A frayed fuse set alight.

Crackling as the heat sizzles,
drenched in haze, left to revive.
The breath lost from the burn,
a shell's edges pushed aside.

Dancing higher before the bang.
Piercing the smoke, new to sight.
Sparking with a colourful bang;
Two new fireworks, lighting up the night.

The Pictures

I hear them giggle in the corners.
The pictures of adolescent innocence,
Hanging their hats on the posts of desires
that railroad responsibilities into spaces.
Where ignorance and arrogance throw shade
upon the faces of coins misspent, on days
that should have been used dangling feet
over fences and playing in paddling pools,
that reflect the hopes of the lost children
and drown the pain of old battles.
Healing the wounds left by inconsistency,
while the meek and the mindful watch on,
hidden behind the shelves of thunder
rocking savagely in the leftover breeze.
They peer around the edges of their frames,
holding tightly to rigidness and rule.
I hear them giggle in the corners,
Those pictures of sophisticated guilt.
At last they break their strings to whisper
"What are you still doing here?"

Insecurity, no. 36

It lingers in my space,
that signature scent of his.
It smells like yellow sweaters
and the parting of our lips.

It stinks like empty vodka bottles.
Perfumes like his nose run through my hair.
Then it burns my throat like cigarettes,
Benson and Hedges in the early Sunday air.

It takes up all my space.
That signature scent of his.
All that I can smell sometimes,
Is Insecurity, no. 36.

Forever Yours, Forever Mine

Your eyes have lost their fire.
It's encased somewhere else in time.
I'll not forget their fond embrace,
Forever Yours, Forever Mine.

Longing can't be innocent.
A crave consumes my soul.
Past sensations light a spark,
it seems logics lost control.

You speak in unsolved riddles
that pain nor pleasure can define.
No-one else will know the thrills.
Forever Yours, Forever Mine.

Our forbidden crimes of passion
ignite the burning flames of lust,
scorch the edges of adoration.
Char the remains of trust.

Murderers we are branded.
Let our bloodied hands entwine.
Consume me with that sinful kiss,
Forever yours, Forever Mine.

Morning Coffee

I dream of the time
when I live every day,
with the same determination
and careless frivolity
that One finds at the bottom,
Of that first morning coffee cup.

Monster

Jekyll?
Can you hear me?
You are lost again inside
this shell of what you should be.
You're the monster, Mr Hyde.

Quiet.
He might hear you.
Screaming that he's lied.
He tells me you don't love me.
You're a monster, Mr Hyde.

Draped

I wear your scars much better than mine.
Perhaps they run deeper?
Scored into the folds of the scarlet cloaks
that drape the great divine
and hide away the smiles.
Biting like ravenous wolves.
Perhaps it is your happy
that's easier to wear than mine.

Bloom

Petals plucked like a forget-me-not.
First I loved, then was forgot.
Forced to wilt in the blazing sun,
feeling like I was the only one.
Left barren and stripped bare.
Planted. Then picked, without a care.

Barely breathing, like a roses smell.
First you inhaled, then cast your spell.
Freed to thrive in brand new soil,
gates like vines left to uncoil.
Deeply rooted in your sun room.
Planted. Then watered. Now I Bloom.

Siren

If your soul screams from the whitewash,

Be thankful that its heart never sank.

For we may be master of our tides

but even big fish can't outgrow their tank.

A list of broken things

The dawns on the new day.
The beginning of New Years.
I add them to the list I write
of many broken things.
Empty vodka bottles
when thrown at the wall.
Records of our favourite song
and a stolen kitchen waltz.
Blanket nest upon the floor.
The thank you silver ring.

Me, since the day we met.
And You; my favourite broken thing.

Rest in Pieces

Hopefully I reached for you.
Dropped our hearts from my hands
but you can only catch yours
and I can only rest among their pieces.

Anxiety

They speak out so clearly.
The voices eight or nine.
Sat around a table
and I wonder which is mine.

One is waving angrily.
Two is holding back the tears.
Three is sitting quietly,
as it has for all these years.

Reading the energy in the room,
Number four just wants a fix.
While number five gets technical
and butts heads with spirited Six.

Seven analyses everything
and is begging for a break.
Eight is singing happily;
Nine battles with heartache.

They all are silences so easily.
The voice eight, no. Nine,
and as they argue around the table,
I realise all of them are mine.

Spilt Milk

Take another sip.
Slip into that place,
space to spiral on your own
alone and drowning in your glass;
vast and bottomless.
Blessed with the numbing,
drumming beat of the edge.
Wedged between happiness and hatred.

Have another drink.
Sink deep into the dark
stark against another day.
Say that this will be your last
glass of poison to regret.
Bet you can do this one more time.
Sigh, repeat the process every try.
I guess you really are what you eat.

It Got Me

I never thought it would be the quiet that would
get me.
The stretching moment of endless silence.
That it would echo like a heartbeat
drumming in your ears
when you're drowning.

I never thought that it would get me.
The weightless burden of eternal soundless
space.
That it would wrap its hands around my neck.
Squeeze the words from my soul so tight
that they st-st-stutter,
stuck in my throat
like a butterfly scared to leave its cocoon.

I never thought it would be the quiet that would
get me.
The useless reasonless waste of time.
That he would clamber in my window
like a thief in the night.
The unapologetic robber, lamenting his return to
my pain
to steal the blankets from the bed of comfort I
had made there.

I never thought that it would get me.
The broken fragments of that misplaced hope.
That she would linger in the doorway
like an unwanted visitor,
leaving one foot in the hallway
then startle from my silent screams
and race fleetingly down the stairs.
Slamming the door in her wake,
announcing she will revisit at another time.

And as she breezed by the confident little
butterfly
beating its battered wings, over and over,
like the ending of an old cinematic film.
Black and White. Black and White. Black and
White.
Marking the end of your beautiful story
and the beginning of the one leftover;
The grief came
and I let it get me.

www.ingramcontent.com/pod-product-compliance
Lightning Source LLC
Chambersburg PA
CBHW061324140726
47998CB00007B/2540